A Maths JOURNEY through the Animal Kingdom

CONTENTS

go figure

You are an intrepid animal scientist and your job is to use your mathematical knowledge to explore some of the wildest parts of the planet, examining the creatures living there.

Learn about expressions, symmetry, place value and other mathematical principles and then use them to solve puzzles that will guide you while you walk on the wild side.

Answers to the Go Figure! challenges can be found on page 28.

Words in *italics* appear in the glossary on page 30.

WHAT EQUIPMENT DO YOU NEED?

You might find some of the questions in this book are too hard to do without the help of a calculator.
Ask your teacher about when and how to use a calculator.

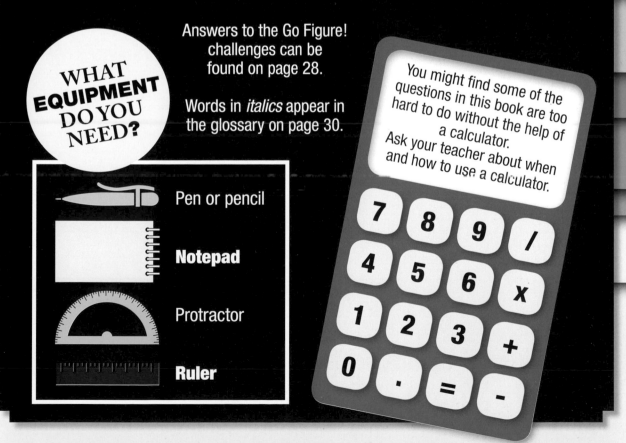

Pen or pencil

Notepad

Protractor

Ruler

ADDING ANTS!

Your first mission is to find out how much anteaters eat in the South American grasslands. However, an anteater has broken into your stores and some ants have gone missing.

LEARN ABOUT IT

ADDING AND SUBTRACTING

04

You can *add* and *subtract* numbers with two, three or more digits by lining them up into columns.

Stack the numbers, one on top of the other, making sure the units (U), tens (T) and hundreds (H) line up:

```
H T U
182 +
274
* * *
```

ADDING
Add the units column first:
2 + 4 = 6

```
182 +
274
* * 6
```

Then add the tens column. Sometimes the total for a column is more than 10:
8 + 7 = 15
Put the '5' at the bottom of the column and carry over the '1', putting it at the top of the next column:

```
1
182 +
274
* 5 6
```

Add the hundreds column, remembering the carried-over number:

```
1
182 +
274
4 5 6
```

SUBTRACTING

We cannot take '3' from '1'. This time, you can borrow 1 from the tens column and take '3' from '11' leaving '8':

$$951^1 - \\ 243 \\ \overline{\quad**8}$$

Don't forget to add the '1' back into the next column:

Now we take (4 + 1) from 5 in the tens column: **5 – 5 = 0**

$$951 - \\ 2^143 \\ \overline{\quad*08}$$

Finally, you can subtract the '2' from the '9' in the hundreds column to complete the sum.

$$951 - \\ 2^143 \\ \overline{\quad708}$$

〉GO FIGURE!

You have counted the number of ants left in your storage boxes and written numbers on the sides.

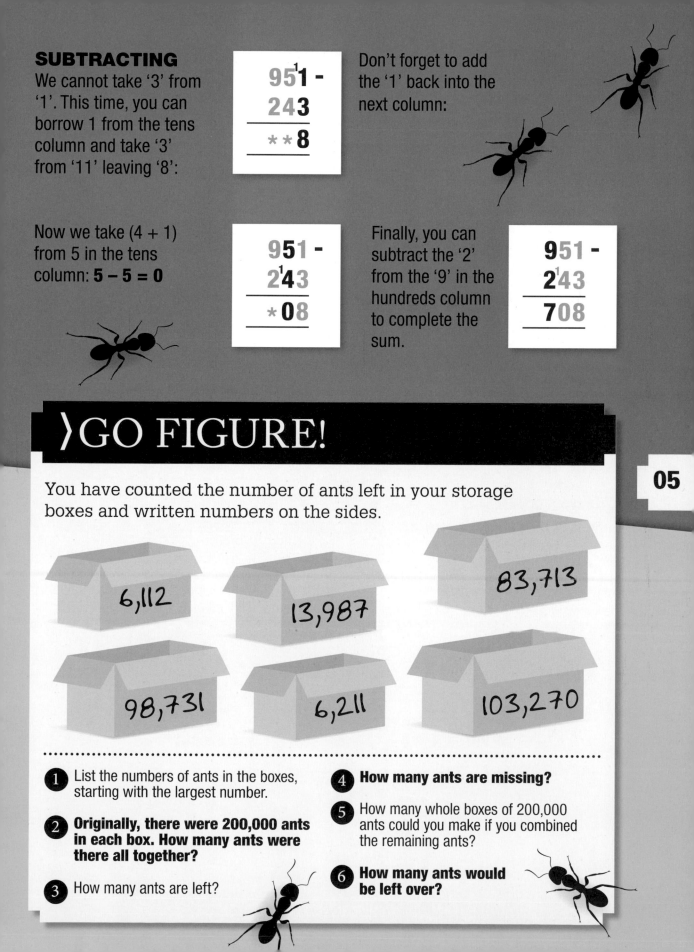

6,112

13,987

83,713

98,731

6,211

103,270

1. List the numbers of ants in the boxes, starting with the largest number.

2. **Originally, there were 200,000 ants in each box. How many ants were there all together?**

3. How many ants are left?

4. **How many ants are missing?**

5. How many whole boxes of 200,000 ants could you make if you combined the remaining ants?

6. **How many ants would be left over?**

QUEST FOR THE JAGUAR

Your next mission takes you to the South American rainforests on the hunt for the jaguar. One has been spotted and your job is to find, track and record the jaguar in action.

LEARN ABOUT IT
PERIMETER AND AREA

The *perimeter* is the distance around the outline of a shape. To work out the perimeter, you have to add up the lengths of all the sides. The *area* of a shape is the space enclosed by it.

To work out the area of a *rectangle*, multiply the length of the short side by the length of the long side. To work out the perimeter of any shape, add up the lengths of all the sides.

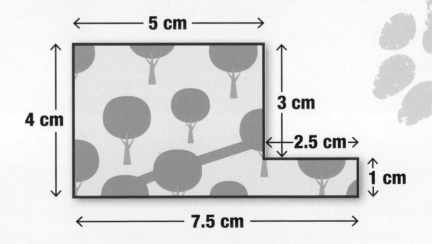

5 cm

4 cm

3 cm

2.5 cm

1 cm

7.5 cm

Perimeter is 4 + 5 + 3 + 2.5 + 1 + 7.5 = 23 cm

Area is made up of 2 rectangles (4 x 5) + (2.5 x 1) = 22.5 cm^2

❯GO FIGURE!

In order to track the jaguar's movements, you need to set up a laser-beam fence around the two areas where the jaguar has been spotted (as shown below). You also need to set up a network of video cameras around the perimeter to record the elusive big cat.

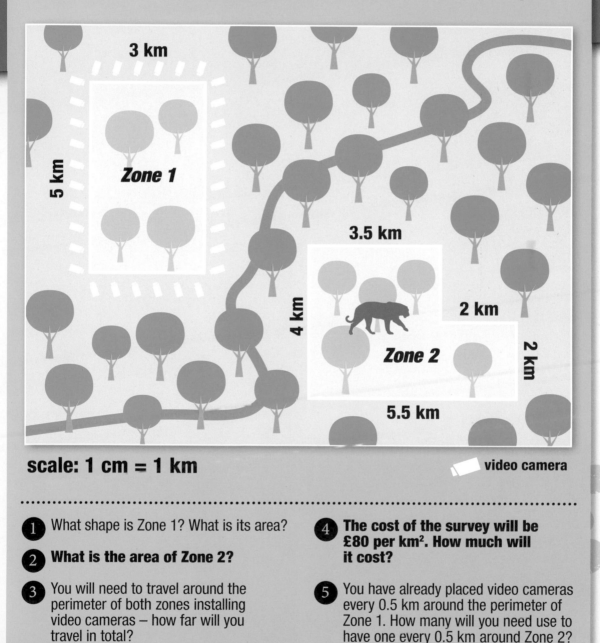

scale: 1 cm = 1 km   📹 video camera

----

1 What shape is Zone 1? What is its area?

2 What is the area of Zone 2?

3 You will need to travel around the perimeter of both zones installing video cameras – how far will you travel in total?

4 The cost of the survey will be £80 per km². How much will it cost?

5 You have already placed video cameras every 0.5 km around the perimeter of Zone 1. How many will you need use to have one every 0.5 km around Zone 2?

FOXES AND HARES

Next, you've travelled to the frozen north to study Arctic foxes and hares. You want to work out how many foxes live in the area you are studying, and you can do that by recording the numbers of Arctic hares over several weeks.

LEARN ABOUT IT
EXPRESSIONS

An *expression* is a way of showing the relationship between numbers. When you don't know a number, you can use a *variable* in its place.

For example, if you use the variable 'h' to stand for the number of hares a fox eats, then the expression '12 x h' or '12h' is the number of hares 12 foxes will eat.

You can use the expression in an *equation* to work out the number you don't know. If you knew 12 foxes ate 36 hares, you could write the equation:

$$12h = 36$$

From this, you can work out that each fox eats three hares – so:

$$h = 3$$

〉GO FIGURE!

You know that a fox will eat four hares each week and your assistant is counting how many hares there are living in the area. Keeping track of the hare population will allow you to calculate the number of foxes.

① There are 'h' hares in 1 km². Write an expression to show how many hares live in 5 km².

② **You discover that there are 180 hares in 1 km². Use your expression to work out how many live in 5 km².**

③ There are 'f' foxes in 1 km². Each fox eats four hares a week. Write an expression to show the number of hares eaten by foxes each week.

④ **There are 180 hares now, and there were 200 hares last week. Write an expression, using your answer to question 3, to show how many foxes there are.**

⑤ Solve your equation.

SNAKE BITE!

On a trip across the desert, you have been bitten by a snake and you need to know if it is venomous. There are four types of snake living in the area, but not all of them are venomous. Which one have you been bitten by?

LEARN ABOUT IT
SYMMETRY

10

A pattern or shape is *symmetrical* when it has parts that are the same when they are either reflected or rotated.

The dotted line is the line of symmetry of this shape. You could fold the shape along the line to make two halves that match exactly. If you put a mirror along the line of symmetry, you will see the same image as if you look at the original shape.

This shape has two lines of symmetry; you could fold it both ways.

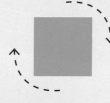

A shape has *rotational symmetry* if you can rotate it and it still looks the same.

A reflected shape is reversed, as though reflected in a mirror.

A rotated shape has been turned around.

⟩GO FIGURE!

Here are the patterns of the four types of snake living in the area. Only one of them is venomous. To find out which one it is, you need to check the patterns on their bodies.

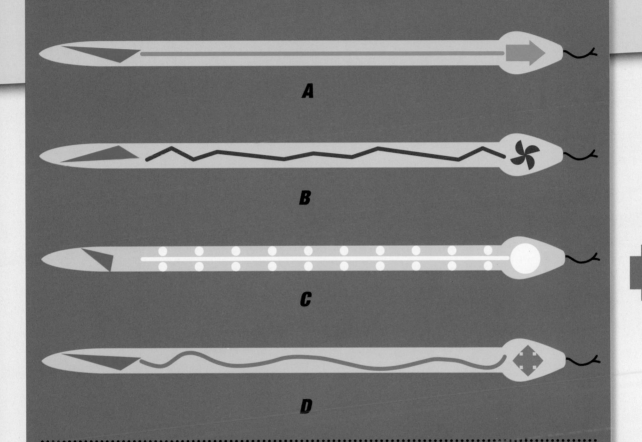

A

B

C

D

1. A venomous snake has a triangle like this at the end of its tail. The triangle can be reflected on the snake's tail, but not rotated. Which snakes have this feature?

2. **A venomous snake also has a symmetrical pattern along its back. Which snakes have this?**

3. Looking at your answers to questions 1 and 2, only one snake has both the head and body markings that show it is a venomous snake. Which one is it?

4. The snake that bit you had a pattern on its head with rotational symmetry. Which of the four snakes have markings on their heads that have rotational symmetry?

5. Comparing all of your answers, was the snake that bit you venomous?

ANTARCTICA ANTICS

Travelling to Antarctica, your next task is to monitor penguin populations. You have found beaches with several penguin nest sites and you have counted all the penguin chicks at each site.

LEARN ABOUT IT
STEM-AND-LEAF PLOTS

Stem-and-leaf plots show the frequency of **values** in a set of **data**. They are arranged as a table with two columns.

Each value is split into two digits, one for the tens and one for the units. The stem column shows the tens figure; the leaf column shows the unit figure.

The number 64 is split like this:

stem	leaf
6	4

To record the values 64, 68 and 63, you would fill in the row like this:

stem	leaf
6	4 8 3

This stem-and-leaf plot shows the number of killer whales spotted at five different locations:

Number of killer whales:

stem	leaf
0	8
1	7
2	3 0
3	1

The values recorded were 8 (08), 17, 23, 20 and 31. There are five values in the leaf column because there were five locations.

〉GO FIGURE!

Your assistant has made a stem-and-leaf plot of the data from the penguin chick survey. Use this to look at the number of chicks at each site.

Number of chicks per nest site:	
stem	leaf
1	8 3
2	9 4 9
3	4 6 7 2
4	5 4 0
5	2 7

1 How many nest sites did you study?

2 **How many sites had between 35 and 60 chicks?**

3 How many chicks were there in total at nests with fewer than 30 chicks?

4 **What is the largest number of chicks at any site?**

5 How many sites had 29 chicks?

6 **What is the total number of chicks in the area?**

TIGER SIGHTINGS

You have arrived in India, where you need to track down tigers for research. They are hard to locate, but you have collected details of sightings from local people and plotted them.

LEARN ABOUT IT
QUADRANTS AND COORDINATES

14

A map or plot can be divided into four *quadrants*. You can refer to any point by giving its *coordinates*. The coordinates are two numbers. The first shows the distance you have to go across on the x-*axis*. The second shows the distance you have to go up or down on the y-axis.

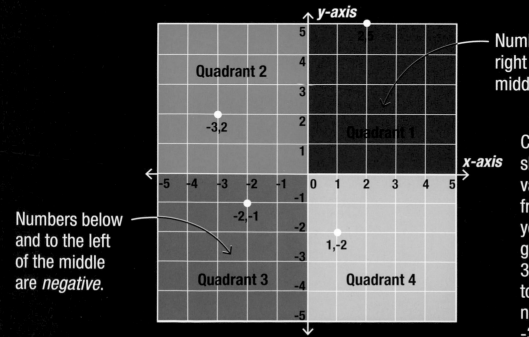

Numbers to the right and above the middle are *positive*.

Coordinates are shown with the x value first. To get from -3,2 to 2,5 you would need to go along 5 and up 3. To get from 1,-2 to -2,-1 you would need to go along -3 and up 1.

Numbers below and to the left of the middle are *negative*.

❭GO FIGURE!

Your assistant has created a map of the area and divided it into four quadrants, using an x-axis and y-axis. Six tiger sightings have been made and their coordinates have been added to the map below.

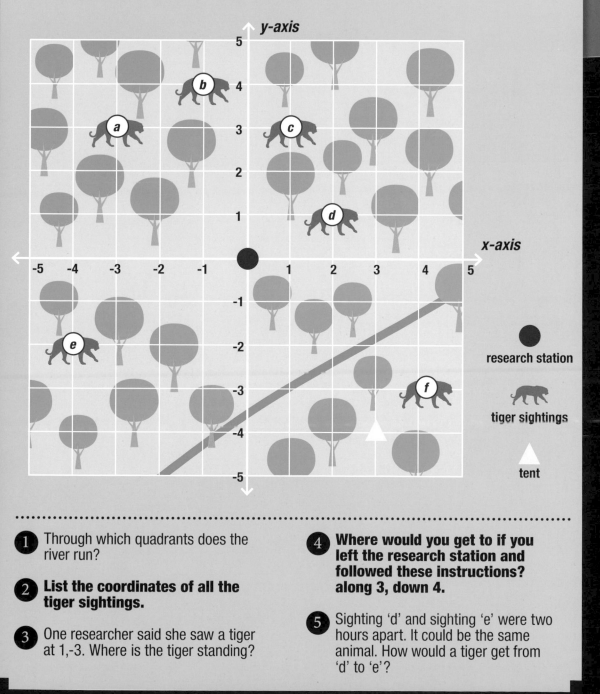

1. Through which quadrants does the river run?

2. **List the coordinates of all the tiger sightings.**

3. One researcher said she saw a tiger at 1,-3. Where is the tiger standing?

4. **Where would you get to if you left the research station and followed these instructions? along 3, down 4.**

5. Sighting 'd' and sighting 'e' were two hours apart. It could be the same animal. How would a tiger get from 'd' to 'e'?

COUNTING FISH

Your next mission is to calculate the number of fish on a coral reef. You are using a radar fish-counting device, which records the numbers of fish using symbols in columns of units, tens, hundreds, and so on.

LEARN ABOUT IT
PLACE VALUE

We use *place value* to show the number of units, tens, hundreds, thousands and so on, that make up a number. We can break numbers down using place value in columns:

16

100,000 Hundred thousands	10,000 Ten thousands	1,000 Thousands	100 Hundreds	10 Tens	1 Units
4	1	3	0	6	9

This number is 413,069 — four hundred and thirteen thousand and sixty-nine. We could write it out as this sum:

$$
\begin{aligned}
400,000 &+ \\
10,000 & \\
3,000 & \\
60 & \\
9 & \\
\hline
413,069 &
\end{aligned}
$$

It is easy to see the place value if we use coloured counters or dots:

100,000 Hundred thousands	10,000 Ten thousands	1,000 Thousands	100 Hundreds	10 Tens	1 Units
••••	•	•••		••• •••	••••• ••••

⟩GO FIGURE!

You have collected data from two zones on the coral reef and your radar device has calculated the total number of fish in each zone.

Zone 1

100,000 Hundred thousands	10,000 Ten thousands	1,000 Thousands	100 Hundreds	10 Tens	1 Units
•		••• •••	••	•	•••• •••

Zone 2

100,000 Hundred thousands	10,000 Ten thousands	1,000 Thousands	100 Hundreds	10 Tens	1 Units
	••		••• ••• •••	••• •••	•••

1. The displays show the total fish for two areas on the reef, Zone 1 and Zone 2. Write the numbers in figures.

2. Copy the table above and draw the correct numbers of symbols for an area in which there were three hundred and forty thousand, seven hundred and twelve fish.

3. Another part of the reef, Zone 3 has fewer fish – there are 11,067 fewer than in Zone 2. Copy out the table and fill in the arrangement of symbols for Zone 3.

4. What is the total number of fish in all three zones. Copy out the table and fill in the display showing the correct symbols for this total?

BIRDS OF PARADISE

You have arrived in the jungle of Borneo to study the territories of Birds of Paradise. You have identified three birds, each of which has its own territory.

LEARN ABOUT IT
TRIANGLES

There are three types of *triangle*:

A *right-angled* triangle is a special sort of scalene triangle. It has one angle that is 90°.

right angle

A scalene triangle has three different sides and three different angles.

The area of a triangle is: **half the base x the height.**

The height is a line drawn at right angles to the base up to the opposite corner.

Sometimes, the height line has to be drawn outside the triangle.

An isosceles triangle has two equal sides and two equal angles.

An equilateral triangle has three equal angles and three equal sides.

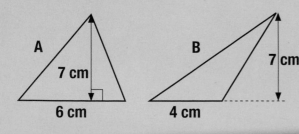

A

7 cm

6 cm

B

7 cm

4 cm

The area of A is ½ x 6 = 3 x 7 = 21 cm²

The area of B is ½ x 4 = 2 x 7 = 14 cm²

The perimeter of a triangle is the sum of its three sides.

⟩GO FIGURE!

You have created a map of the three territories and the triangles they form. Your assistant has also been able to measure the sides of one of the territories.

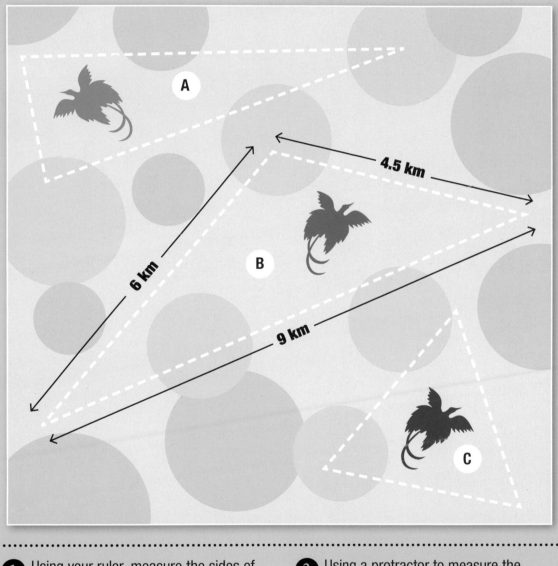

1. Using your ruler, measure the sides of the territories to find out which one is an isosceles triangle?

2. **Which territory has three sides of the same length? What is this type of triangle called?**

3. Using a protractor to measure the angles, which territory has an angle of 20 degrees?

4. **What is the total length of the three sides of Territory B?**

TRACKING SEA TURTLES

You have caught two sea turtles and fitted them with tracking devices. You then let the turtles go in the sea and record where they travel over a 24-hour period.

LEARN ABOUT IT
POLYGONS

20

A *polygon* is a closed shape with straight edges. There are no gaps in its outline. It has corners wherever the edges meet.

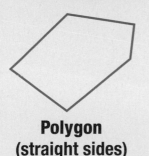

Polygon (straight sides)

Not a polygon (curved side)

Not a polygon (open)

Polygons can be regular or irregular. In a regular polygon, all the sides are the same length and all the angles are equal. Examples of regular polygons are: equilateral triangle, square, regular pentagon, regular hexagon, regular octagon.

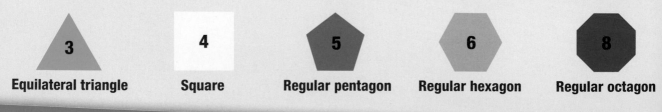

3	4	5	6	8
Equilateral triangle	Square	Regular pentagon	Regular hexagon	Regular octagon

Polygons can have *acute angles*, *obtuse angles* or right-angles. A right-angle is exactly 90°. An obtuse angle is more than 90°. An acute angle is less than 90°.

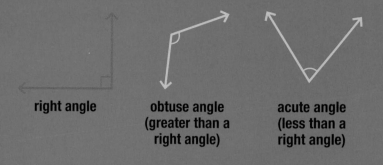

right angle

obtuse angle
(greater than a
right angle)

acute angle
(less than a
right angle)

〉GO FIGURE!

The tracks of the turtles' routes over the last 24 hours are shown on the map below. Each track is made up of a series of straight parts and angles.

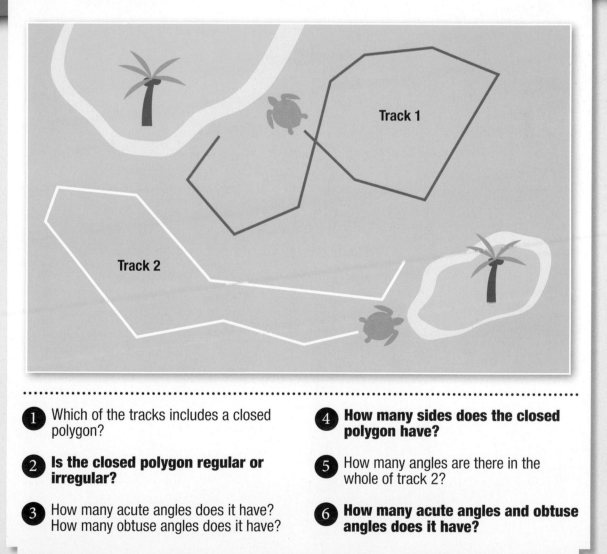

Track 1

Track 2

1 Which of the tracks includes a closed polygon?

2 **Is the closed polygon regular or irregular?**

3 How many acute angles does it have? How many obtuse angles does it have?

4 **How many sides does the closed polygon have?**

5 How many angles are there in the whole of track 2?

6 **How many acute angles and obtuse angles does it have?**

ON THE SAVANNAH

On the African savannah, you have placed video cameras in an area where elephants are known to live. You have used footage of the elephants to calculate their movements.

LEARN ABOUT IT
WORKING WITH TABLES

A *table* is made of boxes, or *cells*, arranged in rows (across the page) and columns (down the page).

22

When you are using data in a table, you might have to look in all the cells to find the biggest or smallest values, or you might have to do calculations using the numbers in the cells. For example, this may involve adding up all the numbers in a column.

	Rhinos	**Zebras**	**Giraffes**
Area 1	11	14	7
Area 2	12	9	3

10   **23**   **23**

From this table, we can see that Area 1 has more animals than Area 2. We can work out that there are 23 rhinos, 23 zebras and 10 giraffes in total.

Information from two video cameras has been used to compile a table. The table shows how many elephants passed by during each period, and the biggest number of elephants that were in shot at any one time during each time period.

TIME	CAMERA 1		CAMERA 2	
	NUMBER OF SIGHTINGS	MOST IN SHOT	NUMBER OF SIGHTINGS	MOST IN SHOT
Midnight–4 am	4	1	5	3
4 am–8 am	7	2	10	4
8 am–12 noon	32	7	45	12
12 noon–4 pm	36	10	53	11
4 pm–8 pm	28	6	23	7
8 pm–midnight	12	3	16	2

23

1 During which time period were elephants most active?

2 Which camera was placed in the area with fewest elephant movements?

3 Looking at the results under 'Most in shot', what is the number that completes this phrase: "There must be at least __ elephants in the area covered by camera 2."

4 Is it possible to tell how many elephants live in the area just from this data?

BREEDING MEERKATS

Still in Africa, you move on to study meerkat family groups. You have learned that most meerkat pairs have litters of three babies. This means a meerkat family usually has five members.

LEARN ABOUT IT

MULTIPLICATION PROPERTIES

When you multiply two numbers together, the order of the numbers doesn't matter. This means that:

$$3 \times 4 = 4 \times 3$$

This is called the *commutative property* of multiplication.

When you multiply three or more numbers together, it does not matter in which order you multiply them. This means that

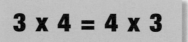

$$3 \times 4 \times 5$$ can be worked out as

$3 \times 4 = 12$		$4 \times 5 = 20$		$3 \times 5 = 15$
then	**or as**	then	**or as**	then
$12 \times 5 = 60$		$3 \times 20 = 60$		$4 \times 15 = 60$

This is called the *associative property* of multiplication.

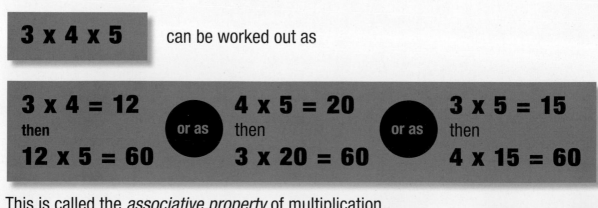

The third property of multiplication is called the *distributive property*. This is because you can distribute or split up numbers into their separate parts. For example:

26 x 6 Can be written as **(20 x 6) + (6 x 6)** or **120 + 36 = 156**

⟩GO FIGURE!

You are studying two zones to calculate the meerkat population in each. Zone A has an area of 7 km², and Zone B has an area of 9 km². There are three meerkat families for every 1 km².

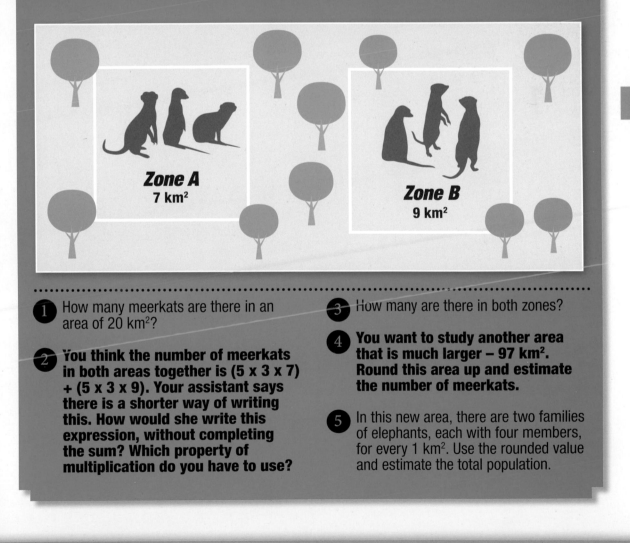

Zone A
7 km²

Zone B
9 km²

1. How many meerkats are there in an area of 20 km²?

2. **You think the number of meerkats in both areas together is (5 x 3 x 7) + (5 x 3 x 9). Your assistant says there is a shorter way of writing this. How would she write this expression, without completing the sum? Which property of multiplication do you have to use?**

3. How many are there in both zones?

4. **You want to study another area that is much larger – 97 km². Round this area up and estimate the number of meerkats.**

5. In this new area, there are two families of elephants, each with four members, for every 1 km². Use the rounded value and estimate the total population.

BUG POPULATIONS

You are in the rainforests of Central Africa, where you have been finding out about the bug population. You have recorded your travel costs observations in tables.

Tables are great ways to study data from different sources. Arranging data in columns allows the figures to be added and compared quickly.

TRANSPORT LOG

MONTH 1	£1,983.67
MONTH 2	£978.11
MONTH 3	£2,034.52
MONTH 4	£1,327.88
TOTAL	£

SCORPION STUDIES

POPULATIONS	
ZONE 1	853
ZONE 2	
ZONE 3	694
TOTAL	2,259

After taking your tent down, it rained and some of your records have been smudged. You will have to work out some of the entries.

OBSERVATION LOG

	START	END	TOTAL TIME
MONDAY	▓	13:31	4 HOURS 14 MINS
TUESDAY	09:16	12:58	▓
WEDNESDAY	▓	13:03	4 HOURS 6 MINS
THURSDAY	7:29	▓	8 HOURS 38 MINS

SPIDER OBSERVATIONS

AREA 1	▓
AREA 2	▓
AREA 3	359
TOTAL	▓

1 Look at the transport log. How much of the budget was spent on transport. Write this down in your notebook.

2 What is the missing number in the scorpion studies list?

3 What are the numbers that have been smudged in the observation log?

4 Your assistant is planning research into spiders. She has kept records of the spiders there are in three areas, but the notes are smudged.

She tells you 'I think there are two hundred and thirty-seven in Area 1 and a hundred and nineteen in Area 2'. Copy out the table and add the missing numbers to complete it.

GO FIGURE! ANSWERS

04-05 Adding ants!
1. 103,270; 98,731; 83,713; 13,987;
   6,211; 6,112
2. 6 x 200,000 = 1,200,000
3. 103,270 + 98,731 + 83,713 + 13,987 +
   6,211 + 6,112 = 312,024
4. 1,200,000 - 312,024 = 887,976
5. Four boxes (800,000 ants)
6. 887,976 - 800,000 = 87,976 ants left

06-07 Quest for the jaguar
1. Zone 1 is a rectangle.
   Its area is 3 km x 5 km = 15 km^2
2. The area of Zone 2 is the sum of the
   area of the rectangle and the area of
   the square
   (3.5 km x 4 km) + (2 km x 2 km) =
   14 km^2 + 4 km^2 = 18 km^2
3. The perimeter of Zone 1 is:
   3 + 5 + 3 + 5 = 16 km
   The perimeter of Zone 2 is:
   4 + 3.5 + 2 + 2 + 2 + 5.5 = 19 km
   So the total perimeter is:
   16 + 19 = 35 km
4. The survey will cost 80 x the total
   area of the two zones:
   80 x (15 + 18) = 80 x 33 = £2,640
5. You need to use 2 cameras for each
   km of perimeter: 19 x 2 = 38 cameras

08-09 Foxes and hares
1. 5h
2. 5h = 5 x 180 = 900 hares in 5 km^2
3. 4f
4. 4f + 180 = 200 OR 200 – 4f = 180
   OR 200 – 180 = 4f
5. 4f = 20, so f = 5;
   there are 5 foxes in the area

10-11 Snake bite!
1. A, B, D
2. A and C
3. A
4. B, C, D
5. No. Snake A is the only snake that is
   venomous and the markings on its
   head do not have rotational symmetry.

12-13 Antarctica antics
1. 14 sites – there are 14 values in the
   leaf column
2. 7: with values 36, 37, 40, 44, 45, 52, 57
3. 18 + 13 + 29 + 24 + 29 = 113
4. 57
5. 2
6. 18 + 13 + 29 + 24 + 29 + 34 + 36 + 37
   + 32 + 45 + 44 + 40 + 52 + 57 = 490

14-15 Tiger sightings

1. 3 and 4
2. a = -3,3; b = -1,4; c = 1,3; d = 2,1;
   e = -4,-2; f = 4,-3
3. The tiger is in the river
4. A tent
5. along -6, down 3

16-17 Counting fish

1. Zone 1: 106,218; Zone 2: 20,653

2.

100,000 Hundred thousands	10,000 Ten thousands	1,000 Thousands	100 Hundreds	10 Tens	1 Units
•••	••••	:•:	•	••

3. 20,653 − 11,067 = 9,586

100,000 Hundred thousands	10,000 Ten thousands	1,000 Thousands	100 Hundreds	10 Tens	1 Units
		::::•	:•	:::	:::

4. 106,218 + 20,653 + 9,586 = 136,457

100,000 Hundred thousands	10,000 Ten thousands	1,000 Thousands	100 Hundreds	10 Tens	1 Units
•	•••	:::	::	::•	:::

18-19 Birds of Paradise

1. A
2. C; equilateral
3. A
4. 9 + 6 + 4.5 = 19.5 km

20-21 Tracking sea turtles

1. Track 1
2. Irregular
3. 1 acute, 6 obtuse
4. 7
5. 8
6. 0 acute, 8 obtuse

22-23 On the savannah

1. 12 noon-4pm: 36 + 53 = 89 sightings
2. Camera 1 with a total of 119 sightings
   (camera 2 had 152 sightings)
3. 12 – at one point between 8 am-
   12 noon there were at least
   12 elephants in shot on camera 2,
   therefore there must be at least
   12 elephants in that area
4. No

24-25 Breeding meerkats

1. 20 km^2 x 3 families x 5 meerkats
   per family = 300
2. 5 x 3 x 16. Distributive
3. 5 x 3 x 16 = 240
4. There are 3 x 5 = 15 meerkats in
   1 km^2, so an estimate would be
   15 x 100 = 1,500 meerkats
5. 2 families x 4 elephants x 100 =
   approximately 800 elephants

26-27 Bug populations

1. £6,324.18
2. 2,259 − (853 + 694) = 712
3.

	START	END	TOTAL TIME
MONDAY	09:17	13:31	4 HOURS 14 MINS
TUESDAY	09:16	12:58	3 HOURS 42 MINS
WEDNESDAY	08:57	13:03	4 HOURS 6 MINS
THURSDAY	7:29	16:07	8 HOURS 38 MINS

4.

AREA 1	237
AREA 2	119
AREA 3	359
TOTAL	715

MATHS GLOSSARY

ACUTE ANGLE
An angle that is less than 90°.

ADD
Combining two numbers to produce a third. If two positive numbers are added, then the resulting number will be bigger.

AREA
The amount of two-dimensional space covered by a shape or object. For example, the area of a rectangle is calculated by multiplying the length of one of the short sides by the length of one of the long sides.

ASSOCIATIVE PROPERTY
The associative property of multiplication means that you can multiply sub-groups in a multiplication sum in any order and the answer will remain the same.

AXIS
A line that is used in maths to locate a point.

CELL
A box in a table into which data and numbers are written.

COMMUTATIVE PROPERTY
The commutative property of multiplication means that you can swap numbers around in a multiplication sum and the answer will remain the same.

COORDINATES
A series of numbers that will locate a point against axes.

DATA
A collection of facts or information.

DISTRIBUTIVE PROPERTY
The distributive property of multiplication means that you can split up numbers into their separate parts in a multiplication sum and the answer stays the same.

EQUATION
An expression that can be solved. An equation has two sides to it that are linked with an equals symbol, or another symbol to show an inequality between the two sides.

EXPRESSION
A way of showing the relationship between two amounts.

NEGATIVE NUMBER
A number that is less than zero.

OBTUSE ANGLE
An angle that is more than 90°.

PERIMETER
The total distance around a shape.

PLACE VALUE
The position of a digit within a number

which defines its value. For example, a three digit number has, from right to left, units, tens and hundreds.

POLYGON
A shape that has three or more sides.

POSITIVE NUMBER
A number that is greater than zero.

QUADRANT
One of the four sections created when a shape is divided by two lines that cross, such as the x-axis and y-axis.

RECTANGLE
A four-sided shape where two sides are longer than the other two and all four corners have an angle of 90°.

RIGHT ANGLE
An angle of 90°.

ROTATIONAL SYMMETRY
A object or shape has rotational symmetry when it can be rotated around a point and it still looks the same.

STEM-AND-LEAF PLOT
A way of showing information and values in different sets. Figures are divided into two columns with the left-hand column containing the stems and the right-hand column containing the leafs.

SUBTRACT
Taking one number away from another to produce a third. If a positive number is subtracted from another positive number, then the resulting number will be smaller.

SYMMETRICAL
When a shape or object has parts that are the same when they are reflected or rotated.

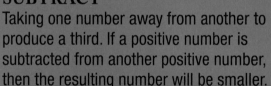

TABLE
A way of laying out numbers and information in rows and columns.

TRIANGLE
A shape with three sides. There are three types of triangle. An equilateral triangle has all three sides and angles the same. An isosceles has two of its sides and angles the same. A scalene triangle has all three sides and angles that are different.

VALUE
The total amount that a number or group of numbers adds up to.

VARIABLE
Something that can have a range of possible values. Variables are usually shown in expressions or equations using a letter or other symbol.

INDEX

WEBSITES

www.mathisfun.com
A huge website packed full of explanations, examples, games, puzzles, activities, worksheets and teacher resources for all age levels.

www.bbc.co.uk/bitesize
The revision section of the BBC website, it contains tips and easy-to-follow instructions on all subjects, including maths, as well as games and activities.

www.mathplayground.com
An action-packed website with maths games, mathematical word problems, worksheets, puzzles and videos.

ACKNOWLEDGEMENTS

Published in Great Britian in 2015 by Wayland
First published in 2014
Copyright © Wayland 2014
All rights reserved.

Dewey number: 510-dc23
ISBN: 9780750289160

10 9 8 7 6 5 4 3 2 1

Wayland
An imprint of Hachette Children's Group
Part of Hodder & Stoughton
Carmelite House
50 Victoria Embankment
London EC4Y 0DZ

Wayland Australia
Level 17/207 Kent Street
Sydney NSW 2000
All rights reserved.

Commissioning editor: Debbie Foy

Produced by Tall Tree Ltd
Editors: Jon Richards
Designer: Ed Simkins
Consultant: Steve Winney

Printed in China
An Hachette UK Company
www.hachette.co.uk
www.hachettechildrens.co.uk